The Rapture
Delusions

BOOKS BY STEVE WOHLBERG

End Time Delusions (book and DVD)

Exposing Harry Potter and Witchcraft

Demons in Disguise:
The Dangers of Talking to the Dead

Hour of the Witch (DVD)

The Trouble With Twilight: Why Today's
Vampire Craze Is Hazardous to Your Health

AVAILABLE FROM DESTINY IMAGE PUBLISHERS

The Rapture
Delusions

Exposing Dangerous Errors
About the End of the World

STEVE WOHLBERG

DESTINY IMAGE® PUBLISHERS, INC.
P.O. Box 310, Shippensburg, PA 17257-0310

"Speaking to the Purposes of God for This Generation and for the Generations to Come."

Previously published six chapters of *End Time Delusions* by Treasure House copyright © 2004   ISBN 0-7684-2960-9

This book and all other Destiny Image, Revival Press, MercyPlace, Fresh Bread, Destiny Image Fiction, and Treasure House books are available at Christian bookstores and distributors worldwide.

For a U.S. bookstore nearest you, call 1-800-722-6774.
For more information on foreign distributors, call 717-532-3040.
Or reach us on the Internet: www.destinyimage.com.

ISBN 10: 0-7684-3209-X
ISBN 13: 978-0-7684-3209-1

For Worldwide Distribution, Printed in the U.S.A.

1 2 3 4 5 6 7 8 9 10 11 / 14 13 12 11 10

*"For this cause God shall send them **strong delusion**, that they should believe a lie."*
—2 Thessalonians 2:11 KJV

Delusion (noun):
1. A misleading of the mind.
2. False belief; a fixed misconception.
3. Something which one accepts as true or real but which is actually false or unreal.

—Webster's New Collegiate Dictionary

A lie can travel halfway around the world before truth puts its boots on.
—Mark Twain (1835-1910)

Table of Contents

Preface

Growing up just over the hill from Hollywood, California, I had absolutely no interest in biblical prophecy for the first 20 years of my life, mainly because I had never heard of such a thing. "Rapture? What's that?" I would have said with a mystified look if you had asked me about it. My Jewish family was warm and friendly but not spiritual. My brother Michael had his bar-mitzvah at age 13, but I didn't, for it was only casually presented to me as a take-it-or-leave-it option. As far as I remember, we never read the Scriptures or prayed even one time.

Some of my young friends perished due to pills and alcohol. It's a miracle I'm not where they are.

As a teenager surrounded by the head-pounding music of rock and roll bands like the Rolling Stones, Aerosmith, and Deep Purple and the drug culture of the 1960s and 1970s, my life took a sharp turn in the wrong direction. Some of my young friends perished due to pills and alcohol. It's a miracle I'm not where they are.

During the summer of 1979, while inhabiting discothèques nightly, I worked as an extra in the film business. One day I was providentially assigned to work on a television series called *From Here to Eternity* on a sandy stretch of Oxnard Beach. There I met a fellow extra who "witnessed" to me about Jesus Christ and the approaching end of the world. With curiosity mingling with interest—and a nagging sense of need for something beyond glamorous illusions—I decided the very next day to visit a Christian bookstore near our home and to scan the prophecy section.

Hal Lindsey's *The Late Great Planet Earth* was the first Christian book I ever touched. I bought it and two of his other books, *Satan Is Alive and Well on Planet Earth* and *Terminal Generation.* Although my marijuana-clouded brain hardly understood what I read, God used those books and started working inside my mind.

A few days later, I found a Bible and began to read. Dimly at first, I slowly started comprehending the message and grace of Jesus Christ. The turning point came when I read about the intense pressure Christ endured in the Garden of Gethsemane, the blood that dripped from His forehead, the appearance of a heavenly angel to strengthen Him, and His unfathomable love for a perishing world (see Luke 22:39-44). After wrestling with a mysterious cup, Jesus made that critical decision—the choice to save lost sinners no matter what it cost Him personally, even if it meant separation from His Father. Finally I read—to use the title of Mel Gibson's hard-hitting film—about *The Passion of the Christ* and His suffering on the Cross. That did it. Shortly thereafter, in a dormitory room at California State University of Northridge, I slipped to my knees and invited my Messiah into my heart. My darkness turned to light! Jesus freely forgave my sins, removed my guilt, and changed my life! No more drugs. I was clean.

After discovering that my Messiah came once as the Babe of Bethlehem, my interest was strongly piqued in the subject of His second coming and the events predicted to occur during Earth's last days. I craved understanding and longed to be ready for the return of the One who was crucified for me, should it occur in my lifetime. This explains my interest in and passion for prophecy.

Could religious leaders *today* be making a similar mistake by misunderstanding the prophecies of *His second coming?*

That was 30 years ago. I've learned a lot since I first read Hal Lindsey's books while working as an extra in Hollywood. One thing that has impressed me for years—and which was so poignantly displayed in Mel Gibson's gripping film—is the reality that one reason why the religious leaders in Christ's day rejected their Messiah was because they misunderstood the Old Testament prophecies predicting His arrival. Think about it. Because it happened once, couldn't it happen again? Could religious leaders *today* be making a similar mistake by misunderstanding the prophecies of *His second coming?* Yes they could, and yes, many are making such a mistake. That's why I wrote *The Rapture Delusion,* which not only proves that massive distortions have entered Christianity but also clarifies much of what the Scriptures actually teach about the end of the world.

Inside these pages I have combined years of research, countless hours of study, and only God knows how many earnest prayers for "the Spirit of truth" to guide me into "all truth" (see John 16:13). I hope the discoveries you are about to make will thrill your heart as they did mine when I first learned them.

Get ready for an amazing journey—controversial for sure, yet exciting and rewarding as well. When Jesus Christ does return, may we all *be found by Him in peace, without spot and blameless*" through His perfect righteousness (2 Peter 3:14).

—Steve Wohlberg

Introduction

It was 4:09 p.m., Eastern Standard Time, on Thursday, August 15, 2003. It started with a blip. Lights flickered and then went out, and in a few hours it was dark from New York to Cleveland to Detroit, even into Canada. The late-August front cover of *Newsweek* labeled the event, "Blackout of 2003." Thankfully, the 50 million North Americans affected took it quite well. Looting was minimal, and no one died.

The Rapture Delusion is about another blackout—a spiritual one—now occurring within Christianity concerning the true meaning of God's *"sure word of prophecy"* (2 Peter 1:19 KJV). Millions of prophecy-minded Christians, including me, sense we are nearing the return of Jesus Christ. Yet when it comes to what the majority *think* is going to happen during Earth's last days and what the Bible *actually says* will occur, the difference is seismic.

It's no secret that the following five teachings have become immensely popular:

1. All true Christians will soon vanish in the rapture.

2. Seven years of apocalyptic terror will overtake those left behind.

3. One sinister man—the antichrist—will take over the world.

4. The antichrist will enter a rebuilt temple in Jerusalem, claiming to be God.

5. The nations of earth will attack Israel at Armageddon.

These five concepts are being taught on radio, on television, at prophecy conferences, in countless books and magazines, in end-time movies, in seminaries, and on the Internet. This five-point belief system is also tightly connected—with one event supposedly leading to the next—just like New York City's electrical power grid is intertwined.

On August 15, 2003, at 4:00 P.M., our nation's generators, electrical cables, transmission lines, and systems operators were all working efficiently together. Everything was fine. Until 4:09. Then a single, high-voltage current forced America into "the largest power outage in our history."[1]

When it comes to popular prophetic theories, is it possible a large portion of Christianity is now in the midst of another outage—*a truth outage?*

When it comes to popular prophet-ic theories, is it possible a large portion of Christianity is now in the midst of another outage—*a truth outage?* The Bible clearly predicts:

> *For the time will come when they will not endure sound doctrine, but according to their own desires, because they have itching ears, they will heap up for themselves teach-ers; and they will turn their ears away from the truth, and be turned aside to fables* (2 Timothy 4:3-4).

Has that time come?

The purpose of *The Rapture Delu-sion* is to closely examine the first two teachings just listed. My larger book,

End Time Delusions, tackles the last three. As you read these eye-opening pages, you will discover irrefutable, high-voltage, New Testament proof of another system failure.

Please read this book prayerfully.

With God's help, I hope to turn some lights on.

Endnote

1. "Blackout of 2003," *Newsweek*, August 25, 2003, 21.

chapter 1

Now You See Them, Now You Don't

If in the last few years you haven't
discarded a major opinion
or acquired a new one, check
your pulse, you may be dead.
—Frank Gelett Burgess (1866-1951)

A lthough the exact word *rapture* isn't in the Bible, millions of prophecy-minded Christians have nevertheless been taught that soon God's Church will disappear from planet Earth without a trace. Headlines are predicted to read: "Multitudes Missing, Chaos Sweeps Globe!" "All Children Have Disappeared!" "Massive Traffic Snarls Due to Evaporated Drivers!" "Planes Crash, Trains Wreck, as Pilots and Engineers Vanish!" Perhaps you've seen bumper stickers reading: "In case of Rapture, this vehicle will be unmanned."

In the last few years, the number-one promoter of the rapture idea has been the *New York Times* bestselling *Left Behind* series, coauthored by Tim LaHaye and Jerry B. Jenkins. A high-speed, 16-book sequence of novels about the end times, *Left Behind* teaches that the return of Jesus Christ takes place in two distinct phases. First, Jesus comes *invisibly* to remove His Church before a seven-year tribulation, during which the rest of humanity must face the antichrist. This is the rapture. At the end of those seven years, Jesus will again return *visibly* to deliver those who became Christians during the tribulation—after being given a "second chance" to be saved—and to pulverize the invading enemies of Israel at Armageddon. This is the second coming. Thus, it's rapture first, then seven years with the antichrist, then the visible second coming of Jesus Christ.

...a rumor has circulated
that some higher-ups at
a large airline want at
least one non-Christian
pilot aboard each flight—
just
in case!

These popular concepts—rapture, seven years of horror, future antichrist—have also been taught in many apocalyptic Christian films, such as *A Thief in the Night*, *Image of the Beast*, *Tribulation Force*, *The Omega Code*, *Left Behind: The Movie*, and *Megiddo*. Because the rapture teaching has been promoted so heavily in our society, even among those outside the Church, a rumor has circulated that some higher-ups at a large airline want at least one non-Christian pilot aboard each flight—just in case!

The real question is: Although "rapture" isn't a biblical word, is the doctrine there? If not, could it be an *end-time delusion?* Let's find out.

First of all, the Bible certainly does teach the exciting truth that Jesus Christ will return for His people. Our Lord Himself said, *"I will come again and receive you to Myself"* (John 14:3). All Christians should believe Christ's promise and long to meet Him on that great day.

But will He come invisibly? Will the Church disappear? Does the Bible really teach vanishing Christians? Without a doubt, the most quoted passage used to support the rapture concept is First Thessalonians 4:17. Lots of Christians know this verse by heart, and it is cited in *Left Behind: The Movie.* There Paul wrote that true believers will someday be *"caught up...in the clouds to meet the Lord in the air"* (1 Thess. 4:17). But does "caught up" mean disappear? Is Paul describing a silent return of Jesus Christ before an apocalyptic seven-year tribulation? We don't need to guess. The answer is in the context, and you don't need to have a four-year degree to grasp the truth.

Will the Church disappear? Does the Bible really teach vanishing Christians?

Have you ever driven down a highway without realizing how fast you were going, and then, when you finally looked down at your speedometer, you thought to yourself, *I'm going too fast and must slow down*? This is what we need to do with First Thessalonians 4. We must slow down and take a full look.

Here is what Paul actually wrote:

For the Lord Himself will descend from Heaven with a shout, with the voice of an archangel, and with the trumpet of God. And the dead in Christ will rise first. Then we who are alive and remain shall be caught up together with them in the clouds to meet the Lord in the air. And thus we shall always be with the Lord (1 Thessalonians 4:16-17).

Rapture promoters interpret "caught up" to mean *disappear* because this view fits their tightly meshed prophetic system, yet it must be admitted that the text doesn't say this.

Rapture teachers interpret this event as silent and secret, yet doesn't it seem rather loud and visible? There is a shout, a voice, a trumpet. Have you ever heard of a silent trumpet? The truth is, First Thessalonians 4:16 is one of the noisiest verses in the Bible! Look carefully: Jesus Christ comes down from Heaven shouting and blowing a trumpet. The dead rise. Then true believers are "caught up." Honestly, do you see anything here about vanishing Christians prior to the tribulation? Rapture promoters interpret "caught up" to mean *disappear* because this view fits their tightly meshed prophetic system, yet it must be admitted that the text doesn't say this.

Two thousand years ago, at the end of His earthly life, Jesus Christ was also "taken up," (see Acts 1:9). This doesn't mean He disappeared, leaving His clothes on earth. Instead, in full view of His wondering disciples, *"while they watched, He was taken up, and a cloud received Him out of their sight"* (Acts 1:9). This event was highly visible. Luke said Jesus Christ was "taken up," and then clouds are mentioned, just like Paul wrote about believers being "caught up…in the clouds."

Notice carefully the full context of this verse:

Now when He had spoken these things, while they watched, He was taken up, and a cloud received Him out of their sight. And while *they looked steadfastly toward Heaven as He went up, behold, two men stood by them in white apparel, who also said, "Men of Galilee, why do you stand gazing up into Heaven? This same Jesus, who was taken up from you into Heaven, **will so come in like manner as you have seen Him go into Heaven**"* (Acts 1:9-11).

Everything will be highly visible, just like the ascension of Jesus Christ.

Here we have holy angels—in the form of men in white robes—explaining the simple truth about Jesus Christ's return. They told the disciples that just as Jesus was literally and visibly "taken up" into the clouds, even so would He *"come in like manner as* [they had] *seen Him go into Heaven."* Although these angels never attended a seminary, there's no doubt they had their theology straight. They taught no secret coming or vanishing Christians. Everything will be highly visible, just like the ascension of Jesus Christ.

Let's return to First Thessalonians and take a look at the thief-in-the-night idea:

> *For the Lord Himself will descend from Heaven with a shout, with the voice of an archangel, and with the trumpet of God. And the dead*

in Christ will rise first. Then we who are alive and remain shall be caught up together with them in the clouds to meet the Lord in the air. And thus we shall always be with the Lord. Therefore comfort one another with these words. But concerning the times and the seasons, brethren, you have no need that I should write to you. For you yourselves know perfectly that the day of the Lord so comes as a thief in the night. For when they say, "Peace and safety!" then sudden destruction comes upon them, as labor pains upon a pregnant woman. And they shall not escape (1 Thessalonians 4:16-5:3).

Here Paul compares the coming of Jesus Christ to the arrival of a midnight thief. Rapture promoters interpret this to mean Jesus will come like a *silent* thief to snatch believers off this earth before seven years of chaos—then driverless cars will crash, pilotless planes will collide, and babies will be found missing from their cribs. The Christian film *A Thief in the Night,* which is similar to *Left Behind: The Movie,* portrays this dramatically. Yet is this really what Paul is saying?

Again, let's slow down and take a closer look at our biblical speedometers. First of all, the day when Jesus comes as a thief is clearly *the very same day* in which He descends with a shout and a trumpet blast. Second, it comes as "a

thief in the night" only upon the unprepared. When it hits, "sudden destruction comes upon them [the lost], as
labor pains upon a pregnant woman.
And they shall not escape."

. . . it is not a secret coming,
but only a sudden one.

Do you see what Paul is really saying?
Jesus' coming as a "thief in the night"
does not mean He will come quietly and
invisibly to steal believers out of this
world, as is taught in rapture movies and
New York Times bestselling books.
Rather, it means He will come unex-
pectedly, bringing "sudden destruction"

upon the unsaved. *Thus, it is not a secret coming, but only a sudden one.* Will the unprepared get a "second chance" to be saved during a subsequent seven-year tribulation? Paul answered this question when he wrote, *"They shall not escape"* (1 Thess. 5:3).

Here's a simple summary of what First Thessalonians 4:16-5:3 really says:

1. Jesus Christ will literally descend from Heaven with a shout and a trumpet blast.

2. The dead in Christ will rise first and true believers will be "caught up," just like Jesus Christ Himself was visibly "taken up" into the sky almost 2,000 years ago.

3. This cataclysmic "day of the Lord" will burst upon the unprepared like the unexpected arrival of a midnight thief.

4. "Sudden destruction" will overwhelm the lost, "and they shall not escape."

When taken literally, these words describe the visible second coming of Jesus Christ, not a secret rapture.

Immediately after his solemn prediction of Christ's return as a midnight thief, Paul wrote to true believers:

But you, brethren, are not in darkness, so that this Day should overtake you as a thief. You are all sons of light and sons of the day. We are

not of the night nor of darkness
(1 Thessalonians 5:4-5).

Remember the Blackout of 2003? It left 50 million North Americans in darkness because a massive system failure short-circuited our electrical power grid. In the prophecy realm, when it comes to popular interpretations of First Thessalonians 4:16-5:3, we have just witnessed another system failure. Honestly, the doctrine of a silent, secret return of Jesus Christ and vanishing Christians *is just not there.*

Again, Paul wrote, *"You are all sons of light and sons of the day. We are not of the night nor of darkness"* (1 Thess. 5:5).

God wants us to avoid truth outages.

He wants the lights on.

chapter 2

The Parousia and Twinkling Eyes

Beware lest you lose the sub-stance by grasping at the shadow.
—Aesop (620-560 B.C.)

Jesus Christ predicted, "Then two men will be in the field: one will be taken and the other left. Two women will be grinding at the mill: one will be taken and the other left. Watch therefore, for you do not know what hour your Lord is coming" (Matthew 24:40-42).

This is probably the second most quoted Scripture in the Bible used to support the doctrine of an invisible return of Jesus Christ and vanishing Christians. Supposedly, *"one will be taken and the other left"* means believers will disappear in an unperceived flash, while the rest of the world suddenly wakes up in mystified ignorance wondering, *Which way did they go?*

Again, the key is in the context. Matthew 24 begins with our Savior quietly sitting upon the Mount of Olives. His *"disciples came to Him privately, saying,*

'Tell us, when will these things be? And what will be the sign of Your coming, and of the end of the age?'" (Matt. 24:3) Obviously, the disciples were thinking about Jesus' return and the end of the world. Because of mental gaps and some loose ends, they asked the Master to clarify the truth.

Before we look at Christ's response, notice the little word *coming* in verse 3. The original Greek word there is *parousia*—you can check it in any good concordance. While you don't need to be a Greek scholar to understand the Bible, that small word is of large importance. As we shall soon see, the "parousia principle" will soon provide vital insights into the rapture question.

...when it comes to this exact topic of His "coming" or parousia, Jesus knew there was going to be a great deal of deception whirling around.

In response to His disciples' please-clarify-the-end inquiry, Christ's very first words were, *"Take heed that no one deceives you"* (Matt. 24:4). The forcefulness of this response should hit us like a hurricane! Why? Because it clearly implies that when it comes to this exact topic of His "coming" or *parousia,* Jesus knew there was going to be a great deal of deception whirling around. And what is even more dramatic is that Christ raised His "Don't Be Deceived" warning flag *four times* in this single sermon (see Matt. 24:4-5,11,24). One gets the idea that *prophecy delusions* will someday sweep over planet Earth like a massive tidal wave. The only way to avoid being swept away in this swirling sea of falsehood is to pay close attention to the exact words of Jesus Christ.

Our Lord continued, *"For false christs and false prophets will rise and show great signs and wonders to deceive, if possible, even the elect"* (Matt. 24:24). Here Jesus said satan's delusions will eventually become so subtle and powerful that only "the elect" will come through unscathed. Who are "the elect"? Based on the context, they must be a group of people who know the Truth-teller and the Bible so well that even the devil can't mislead them. Verse 31 also tells us that "the elect" are people who are ready for the return of Jesus Christ.

Who are "the elect"? Based on the context, they must be a group of people who know the Truth-teller and the Bible so well that even the devil can't mislead them.

Immediately after warning about tricky false prophets and deception, Jesus said:

*Wherefore if they shall say unto you, Behold, He is in the desert; go not forth: behold, He is in the **secret** chambers; believe it not. For as the lightning cometh out of the east, and shineth even unto the west; so shall also the coming of the Son of Man be* (Matthew 24:26-27 KJV).

Here Jesus draws a razor-sharp contrast between false views of His return and the truth.

How should we respond to the idea of a secret return?

Concerning false views, don't miss that little word— *secret* (see Matt. 24:26). Jesus plainly warned that some will mistakenly promote a "secret" coming. Based on the context, we discover that this will be one of those powerful delusions that only God's faithful elect will avoid. How should we respond to the idea of a secret return? Christ's answer is stunning. *"Believe it not."* Why? Because *"as the lightning comes from the east and flashes to the west, so also will the coming of the Son of Man be"* (Matt. 24:27).

When it comes to the parousia, Jesus clarified it would be *anything but secret.*

Far from being a secret event, Jesus Himself compares His return to the brilliant flashing of electric bolts of lightning hurtling across the sky. Now here's an important point. Guess what exact Greek word Matthew used for "coming" in verse 27? The same one he used in verse 3—*parousia.* This is clear evidence that the parousia definitely applies to the highly visible second coming of Jesus Christ. In Hollywood action movies, hidden files are sometimes labeled, "Top Secret." When it comes to the parousia, Jesus clarified it would be *anything but secret.*

Christ's bewildered disciples had inquired, *"…what will be the sign of Your coming* [the parousia], *and of the end of the age?"* After warning about secretive delusions, Jesus finally answered their exact question by lifting the curtain of history and fully unveiling what His cataclysmic return would be like:

And then shall appear the sign of the Son of Man in Heaven: and then shall all the tribes of the earth mourn, and they shall see the Son of Man coming in the clouds of Heaven with power and great glory. And He shall send His angels with a great sound of a trumpet, and they shall gather together His elect from the four winds, from one end of Heaven to the other (Matthew 24:30-31 KJV).

This description of Jesus Christ's return contains more punch than the highly speculative, evolutionary big bang theory. There's no question about it. His "coming," or parousia, will be unmistakably *visible* to "all the tribes of the earth." The dazed masses of humanity will literally "*see* the Son of Man coming in the clouds of Heaven with power and great glory." Certainly no one will miss it, and no one will wake up the next day wondering, *Which way did the Christians go?* On that awesome day, the unsaved will "mourn." Why? Because their loved ones have vanished? No! But because Jesus Christ has *suddenly come* and their last chance for preparation is behind them. Now it's too late. They're lost forever.

There's no question about it. His "coming," or parousia, will be unmistakably *visible* to "all the tribes of the earth."

This entire passage also parallels Paul's words in First Thessalonians 4:16-17. Just like in Paul's description of what will happen when true believers are "caught up," Jesus Christ also said His coming would be a very noisy event that will include loud reverberations from "a great sound of a trumpet" throughout the sky. When that booming blast is heard, multitudes of shining angels will descend into Earth's polluted atmosphere, circle the globe, and "*gather together* His elect from the four winds, from one end of Heaven to the other." Thus true believers will be "caught up" into the air. Now don't miss it. These are the very same elements Paul wrote about in First Thessalonians 4:17!

**Jesus Christ also said
His coming would be
a very noisy event…**

In *both* Matthew 24:30-31 and in First Thessalonians 4:16-17, we read about clouds, noise, a loud trumpet, a gathering together, and true believers being transported into the sky. When we place these sections side by side—without prejudice or preconceived ideas—the message is unavoidable, inescapable, and irrefutable. Both passages refer to the loud, climactic, highly visible, and glorious second coming of Jesus Christ!

Back to Matthew 24; the Truth-teller continued:

> *But of that day and hour no one knows, not even the angels of Heaven, but My Father only. But as the days of Noah were, so also will the coming of the Son of Man be. For as in the days before the flood, they were eating and drinking,*

marrying and giving in marriage, until the day that Noah entered the ark, and did not know until the flood came and took them all away, so also will the coming of the Son of Man be. Then two men will be in the field: one will be taken and the other left. Two women will be grinding at the mill: one will be taken and the other left. Watch therefore, for you do not know what hour your Lord is coming. But know this, that if the master of the house had known what hour the thief would come, he would have watched and not allowed his house to be broken into. Therefore you also be

*ready, for the Son of Man is com-
ing at an hour you do not expect*
(Matthew 24:36-44).

Here Jesus Christ compared His
return to the sudden descent of billions of tons of water upon lost sinners in Noah's day. Those ancient
people thought Noah was a crazy old
man, until *"the flood came and took
them all away, so also will the **coming** of
the Son of Man be"* (Matt. 24:39).
Guess what Greek word is used here
again for "coming"? Don't take my
word for it; look in your own concordance. It's *parousia*, which, as we have
already proven, unmistakably applies
to the highly visible second coming of
Jesus Christ.

**Here Jesus Christ com-
pared His return to the
sudden descent of billions
of tons of water upon
lost sinners in Noah's day.**

Now notice, *immediately* after Jesus
described His parousia in verse 39, He
continued without skipping a beat:
*"Then two men will be in the field: one
will be taken and the other left"* (Matt.
24:40). Remember, this is the second
most widely quoted verse used to but-
tress the secret rapture doctrine. Supposedly, when verse 40 is fulfilled, those
who are "taken" will vanish without a

trace, leaving only their clothes, shoes, false teeth, and wedding rings, while those who are "left" will have to endure a horrific seven-year tribulation and face the antichrist. But is this really what Jesus Christ is saying?

We all should open our own Bibles, pick up our own concordances, and find out for ourselves what truth is.

We don't need to depend on scholars to find the answer. In fact, it is never safe to lean completely on any man, no matter how smart or educated they may be. Christians should never be taught to rely solely on Tim LaHaye, John Walvoord, Thomas Ice, Hal Lindsey, Jack Van Impe, Grant Jeffrey, Chuck Smith, John Hagee, or any other popular teacher, including Steve Wohlberg. We all should open our own Bibles, pick up our own concordances, and find out for ourselves what truth is. If you are willing to do it, here is what you will surely find: Believers will be "taken" at the "coming," or *parousia,* which the Bible clearly applies to the loud, visible, and glorious appearance of Jesus Christ at the very end of the world (see Matt. 24:3,27,30-31,39-40).

Jesus basically said, "It will be just like Noah's day" (see Matt. 24:37-39). Now think about it. Did Noah and his family vanish before the flood? No, they walked visibly into the ark. And what about those who were *left behind* after the door of the ark was shut? Did they have a second chance? No again. How were they left? *They were left dead; they did not escape.* After saying, "the flood came, and took them all away," Jesus made His power-packed point, *"so also will the coming* [parousia] *of the Son of Man be"* (Matt. 24:39). And then, without a break, Christ said, *"**Then** two men will be in the field: one will be taken and the other left"* (Matt. 24:40). Upon careful analysis, these words leave no room for *Left Behind's* tantalizing saga about "tribulation believers" resisting the antichrist during a post-rapture seven-year period. Why not? Because those who are "taken" are transported up at the "coming," or *parousia,* which applies to the *final* second coming of Jesus Christ!

…what about those who were *left behind* after the door of the ark was shut? Did they have a second chance?

Immediately after saying, *"One will be taken and the other left,"* the King of kings then compared His second coming to the sudden arrival of a midnight thief, just like Paul did in First Thessalonians 5:2-3. Jesus Christ said:

But know this, that if the master of the house had known what hour the thief would come, he would have watched and not allowed his house to be broken into. Therefore you also be ready, for the Son of Man is coming at an hour you do not expect (Matthew 24:43-44).

. . . watch out for satanic temptations and end-time delusions.

To "watch" doesn't mean spending endless hours in front of the television set, nor does it mean watching popular movies about the end times that take detours away from the straight truth.

Rather, it means to *watch out for satanic temptations and end-time delusions.*

Matthew 24 and First Thessalonians 4 and 5 fit together just as perfectly as Adam and Eve before they sinned. Both describe a noisy, highly visible, trumpet-blasting, glorious return of Jesus Christ in the clouds. Both describe believers being transported into the air.

True believers are urged to watch, be ready, and to avoid all subtle, secretive, devilish tricks.

Both declare this day will come with thief-like suddenness upon all sleeping sinners. In Noah's day, when billions of tons of water came crashing down, there were no second chances for those who refused to enter the ark. Similarly, Paul said the lost "shall not escape." And both Paul and Matthew use the same Greek word to describe this great and awesomely powerful "day of the Lord." Look in your own concordance. It's *parousia,* which clearly refers to Christ's second coming. True believers are urged to watch, be ready, and to avoid all subtle, secretive, devilish tricks.

Before we close this chapter, let's look at one more passage describing an event predicted to occur *"in a moment, in the twinkling of an eye"* (see 1 Cor. 15:52). This is probably the third most quoted pro-rapture verse used to support the idea of vanishing Christians prior to a nightmarish seven-year tribulation. We have previously slowed down to look at our biblical speedometers, yet this time we must come to a screeching halt. Context, context, context—that's the safety zone. Notice carefully what Paul really wrote:

> *Behold, I tell you a mystery: We shall not all sleep, but we shall all be changed—in a moment, in the twinkling of an eye, **at the last trumpet. For the trumpet will sound**, and the dead will be raised incorruptible, and we shall be changed* (1 Corinthians 15:51-52).

Is Paul saying believers will someday vanish while their loved ones blink? Not at all! He is simply saying that the dead will be raised and our sinful bodies will be changed *"in a moment, in the twinkling of an eye." When* will this "moment" take place? Paul's answer is clear. It will occur "at the *last* trumpet," when "the trumpet will sound," that is, at the very end of the world. This is the very same "great sound of a trumpet" Jesus Christ said would be heard when He finally commissions His shiny angelic friends to gather His people at His second coming (see Matt. 24:31).

Is Paul saying believers will someday vanish while their loved ones blink? Not at all!

In summary, the parousia principle (supported by the context of Matthew 24) proves the "one will be taken" event occurs at the final second coming of Jesus Christ. And based on the full context of First Corinthians 15:52, *"the twinkling of an eye"* moment similarly occurs at the very end of the age.

Around April 15, even Christians sometimes need to file tax return extensions with the Internal Revenue Service. I've done this myself. Such extensions are allowed and usually approved. But to add a seven-year extension to Jesus Christ's words in Matthew 24:40, or to Paul's message in First Corinthians 15:52 is, quite frankly, a *rapture delusion*.

A certain minister acquired a reputation for telling his church members, "It could be worse," during times of great trial. One day a troubled soul told the pastor, "Last night I dreamed Jesus came on the clouds with shiny angels.

The most horrible thing was, I was lost!" Expecting encouragement, the minister shockingly replied, "It could be worse." *What!* thought the man in disbelief. *What could be worse?* Solemnly his pastor whispered, "It would be worse if it wasn't a dream."

How true! Thankfully, the loving arms of Jesus Christ are still open to lost sinners. Let's respond to God's goodness and the pleading voice of the Crucified One before His visible return *is not a dream.*

...the loving arms of
Jesus Christ are still
open to lost sinners.

chapter 3

Will God's Church Escape Tribulation?

*The brightest crowns that are worn
in Heaven have been tried, and
smelted, and polished and glorified
through the furnaces of tribulation.*
—Edwin Hubbel Chapin (1814-1880)

These two concepts come with the rapture package:

1. The Church of Jesus Christ will escape the "tribulation."

2. Those who miss the rapture will have a second chance to be saved.

…by adopting a lazy "let's wait and see" attitude, lost sinners may *put off their decision* to repent and follow Jesus Christ right now.

Apart from what the Bible actually teaches about number one, if you think about it, number two *can* be dangerous. Some might rationalize, "If the rapture takes place, then I'll know God is real. Even though it may be tough, I can still become a Christian during the tribulation and resist that antichrist guy!" In this way, by adopting a lazy "let's wait and see" attitude, lost sinners may *put off their decision* to repent and follow Jesus Christ right now.

Yet historically, God's people have gone through intense suffering.

Die-hard, pretribulation supporters sometimes say, "God wouldn't allow His people to go through the tribulation. He loves us too much!" But think about it. Does He love us any more than He would love after-the-rapture new believers during the tribulation? No. Then why would He allow them to go through such a horrific period but not us? Could it be that the idea of *escaping tribulation* is really only catering to our lukewarm American tendencies? We like comfort, hate to go through trials, and can hardly bear it when our television-dinner lifestyle is threatened. Yet historically, God's people have gone through intense suffering. All the disciples of Jesus except John were brutally murdered. Thousands of early Christians were torn to shreds by wild dogs inside the Coliseum. Millions of others were horribly tortured by the Inquisition and burnt to ashes during the Dark Ages. Believers in Russia and China have suffered terribly under communism and so have many faithful followers of Christ in some Muslim countries, yet many American prophecy experts still contend, "God wouldn't allow *us* to go through the tribulation!"

Really?

In the light of these Scriptures, the idea of Christians escaping tribulation seems like fantasy and illusion.

When it comes to "tribulation," once again concordances come in handy. If you look up *tribulation* in *Strong's* or *Young's Concordance*, you may be shocked to discover that almost every reference describes what believers suffer *through.* Jesus told His followers, ... *"In the world you will have tribulation"*... (John 16:33). Paul told his early Christian converts, *"...we must through many tribulations enter the Kingdom of God"* (Acts 14:22). Paul wrote to the church at Thessalonica, *"...we ourselves boast of you among the churches of God for your patience and faith in all your persecutions and tribulations that you endure"* (2 Thess. 1:4). On the lonely isle of Patmos, John was our *"companion in the tribulation"* (Rev. 1:9). Jesus told His church in Smyrna, *"I know your works* [and] *tribulation..."* (Rev. 2:9). In the light of these Scriptures, the idea of Christians escaping tribulation seems like fantasy and illusion.

Some might respond by saying, "Yes, but those verses are talking about 'tribulation,' not *'the* tribulation.'" Again, just think about it. If the majority of the Bible's "tribulation texts" refer to what believers *go through,* why would God's Word suddenly shift gears by teaching that *"the* tribulation" is something believers will *not* go through? Even in *Left Behind,* there are after-the-rapture Christians who go through *"the* tribulation." Jerry B. Jenkins calls them "the Tribulation Force." Therefore the thought of Christians going through this period is not so strange.

If the majority of the Bible's "tribulation texts" refer to what believers *go through*, why would God's Word suddenly shift gears by teaching that *"the* tribulation" is something believers will *not* go through?

Many pro-rapture advocates also argue, "If the Church is going through the tribulation, then why isn't the Church mentioned after Revelation 4?"

Let's take a closer look. In Revelation 4:1, John was told to "come up here." People conclude this represents the rapture and they think the Church isn't mentioned anymore. First of all, John did not actually go to Heaven in Revelation 4:1; he was simply taken up *in a vision,* while his toes remained on Patmos. Second, the Church *is* on earth after Revelation 4. How do we know this? Because Revelation says the beast will make "war with *the saints,*" then we read about "*the faith of the saints*" and finally, during the mark of the beast crisis, the apocalypse refers to "*the saints*" who keep "*the faith of Jesus*" (see Rev. 13:7,10; 14:12).

Some may respond by saying, "Those are the tribulation saints after the rapture, not the Church." But consider this. Paul wrote his New Testament letters to the *"churches of the saints"* (1 Cor. 14:33). What does this tell us? Wherever there are saints, *there is the Church!* Even if the saints mentioned in Revelation 13 and 14 are only the tribulation saints after the rapture, wouldn't they, as sincere believers in Jesus Christ, *still be the Church?*

Wherever there are saints, *there is the Church!*

Rapture teachers contend the Church won't be here for Armageddon. Is this true? The word *Armageddon* is used only once in the entire Bible, in Revelation 16:16, which is the great chapter about the falling of the seven last plagues. Right before verse 16, *during* the time of the plagues, Jesus Christ thunders:

> *"Behold, I am coming as a thief. Blessed is he who watches, and keeps his garments, lest he walk naked and they see his shame." And they gathered them together to the place called in Hebrew, Armageddon* (Revelation 16:15-16).

Did you catch that? Who is Jesus talking to? To the Church! At the time of verse 15, *while* the seven plagues are falling, which is definitely *during* the tribulation, and *right before* the battle of Armageddon, Jesus Christ has not yet come as a thief! Therefore He must come like a thief *at* Armageddon, *after* the tribulation, and this must be the time when He comes to gather His Church.

Like a good commanding officer, Paul urged the soldiers of the Cross, *"Therefore take up the whole armor of God, that you may be able to withstand in the evil day, and having done all, to stand"* (Eph. 6:13). We are to stand in "the evil day." How can we, if we have previously disappeared? Jesus Christ also said, *"But he who endures to the end shall be saved"* (Matt. 24:13). How long must we endure? *To the end.*

**God has given every
one of us more than
"a second chance."**

What about the "second chance" idea? First of all, God has given every one of us more than "a second chance." When we sin and resist His love, the Lord doesn't give up easily. Instead, He gives us countless chances to make a full surrender to His grace. At this very moment, the message of the Gospel is continually sounding to sinners, *"Christ died for our sins;" "Believe on the Lord*

Jesus Christ, and you will be saved;" "*Repent, and believe in the Gospel*" (1 Cor. 15:3; Acts 16:31; Mark 1:15). But eventually, God's patience will wear out and the Angel of Mercy will take his final flight. Humanity will then have passed "the hidden boundary between God's patience and His wrath."[1]

If you are not "caught up" when the Lord descends from Heaven with a shout, you will have blown it big time, forever.

Paul wrote that all who are not fully on the Lord's side when true believers are *"caught up...shall not escape"* (1 Thess. 4:17; 5:3). For them, their second, third, tenth, and ten-thousandth chances are over. Jesus also said, *"But as the days of Noah were, so also will the coming of the Son of Man be"* (Matt. 24:37). After the door of the ark closed, all desperate attempts to get inside were useless. It was too late. Paul also wrote, *"**Now** is the day of salvation"* (2 Cor. 6:2). Friend, this is it. Don't put off your decision to yield your heart 100 percent to Jesus and His love. If you are not "caught up" when the Lord descends from Heaven with a shout, you will have blown it big time, forever.

...fear—fear of the beast
and its mark—often
underlies many desperate
efforts to maintain the
shaky pretribulation
rapture position.

Here's one more key thought before we close this chapter. If the pretribulation rapture doctrine is false, this obviously means we ourselves—if we are alive at that time—must not only pass through earth's final tribulation, but must also face the antichrist and his deadly mark (see Rev. 14:9-10). Here's the biggest problem. Many Christians are deeply afraid of this. Thus, it seems that *fear*—fear of the beast and its mark—often underlies many desperate efforts to maintain the shaky pretribulation rapture position.

This reminds me of the tragic deaths of 118 crewmen inside the giant Russian nuclear submarine, *Kursk*. On Saturday, August 12, 2000, way out in the icy waters of the Barents Sea, east-northeast of Moscow, something went terribly wrong. An explosion took place, followed by another. The "catastrophe developed at lightning speed," and the doomed sub quickly sank to the bottom of the ocean.[2] *Newsweek* ran a story on this called, "A Cry from the Deep." Twenty-three Russians survived the initial blasts and flooding. A letter was later found by deep-sea divers inside a pocket of the one of the corpses. "There are 23 people here… None of us can get to the surface."[3] Because help didn't come quickly enough, they all died. As I have thought about this horrible tragedy, I can imagine *the feeling of fear* in the hearts of those hopelessly trapped Russian sailors deep down below the calm surface of the water.

From what I've seen, fear also often lurks below the pretribulation rapture doctrine. Deep down underneath the surface of many arguments lies the hidden scary thought of having to endure the time of trouble and face the beast. This fear may be unconscious, yet often it is there, and it seems to prevent people from being open-minded enough to even consider another viewpoint. Emotions fly high and many refuse to reasonably examine the clear scriptural evidence in favor of a post-tribulation gathering of the Church to Jesus Christ.

Deep down underneath the surface of many arguments lies the hidden scary thought of having to endure the time of trouble and face the beast.

Sadly, the pretribulation rapture doctrine has become "the great evangelical escape clause for the avoidance of the end times."[4] And for those who *must* have it this way, no amount of evidence will convince them otherwise. Like a triple-bolted door in downtown New York, they are simply closed to the facts. The result? *Truth is left behind.*

> …the pretribulation rapture doctrine has become "the great evangelical escape clause for the avoidance of the end times."

Christians should learn a lesson from popular bumper stickers and trendy T-shirts that say "No Fear." The truth is that we don't need to be afraid, for Jesus Christ has promised, *"I am*

with you always, even to the end of the age" (Matt. 28:20). *"God has not given us a spirit of fear, but of power and of love and of a sound mind"* (2 Tim. 1:7).

Afraid of the dark, a little girl once asked her father if she could sleep in his bedroom. "Of course, honey," he replied.

Lying next to him with the lights out, she was still afraid. "Daddy, is your face turned toward me?"

"Yes dear, now go to sleep."

Even so should we trust our heavenly Father during earth's final days—even when darkness reigns.

Endnotes

1. J. Addison Alexander, "The Doomed Man," qtd. in S. Miller Hageman, comp., *The Princeton Poets* (Princeton, NJ: Princeton University Press, 1879), 79.

2. "A Cry from the Deep," *Newsweek* (November 6, 2000), 43.

3. Ibid.

4. Steve Wohlberg, *End Time Delusions* (New York: Treasure House, 2005), 36.

chapter 4

The Seven-Year
Tribulation Theory

*A man who has committed a
mistake and doesn't correct it
is committing another mistake.*
—Confucius (551-479 B.C.)

If what this book teaches so far is true,
then what about "the seven years"?
The concept of a seven-year period of

tribulation is actually *the underlying foundation* of the entire *Left Behind* scenario (and all other pro-rapture books and movies). Again, the theory is rapture *first*, then seven years of horror.

Book Two of the *Left Behind* novels declares, "The disappearances have ushered in the seven-year period of Tribulation" (*The Tribulation Force,* inside cover). Book Three reveals, "…the seven-year Tribulation is nearing the end of its first quarter…" (*Nicolae,* inside cover). Book Six tells us, "It's the midpoint of the seven-year Tribulation" (*The Indwelling,* inside cover). Book Eight begins with, "…the dawn of the second half of the seven-year Tribulation" (*The Mark,* inside cover). Book Eleven opens "six years into the

Tribulation, two and one-half years into the Great Tribulation" (*Armageddon,* page vii). Thus, this *New York Times, USA Today,* and *Wall Street Journal* bestselling series of end-times prophecy books, endorsed by well-respected church leaders worldwide, is built entirely around this seven-year framework.

Where does this "seven-year" concept come from, anyway? It may shock you, but if you look for "seven years of tribulation" in any concordance, you won't find it. The truth is, from Genesis to Revelation, there is no exact passage that specifically mentions a seven-year period of tribulation at all. Amazingly, the entire theory is really based on a rather speculative interpretation of two little words in one single verse. The text is Daniel 9:27, and the two words are "one week." Let me explain.

...from Genesis to Revelation, there is no exact passage that specifically mentions a seven-year period of tribulation at all.

The Book of Daniel was written while the Jews were in Babylon, in exile because of their sins. Daniel 9:24-27 contains a prophecy from the angel Gabriel to encourage the Jewish people that they would be given a "second chance" to return to Jerusalem, rebuild their Temple, and ultimately, receive their Messiah, Jesus Christ.

This highly controversial prophecy literally reads:

Seventy weeks are determined upon thy people and upon thy holy city, to finish the transgression, and to make an end of sins, and to make reconciliation for iniquity, and to bring in everlasting righteousness, and to seal up the vision and prophecy, and to anoint the most Holy. Know therefore and understand, that from the going forth of the commandment to restore and to build Jerusalem unto the Messiah the Prince shall be seven weeks, and threescore and two weeks [62 weeks]: the street shall be built again, and the wall, even in troublous times. And after threescore and two weeks shall Messiah be cut off, but not for himself: and the people of the prince that shall come shall destroy the city and the sanctuary; and the end thereof shall be with a flood, and unto the end of the war desolations are determined. And he shall confirm the covenant with many for one week: and in the midst of the week he shall cause the sacrifice and the oblation to cease, and for the overspreading of abominations he shall make it desolate, even until the consummation, and that determined shall be poured out upon the desolate (Daniel 9:24-27 KJV).

Thus we have a prophecy about "seventy weeks." Gabriel then subdivides the period into three smaller periods of seven weeks, sixty-two weeks, and one week. Seven plus sixty-two plus one equals seventy.

Seventy weeks equals 490 days. A day in prophecy represents a year (see Num. 14:34 and Ezek. 4:6). Thus 490 days are really 490 years. Without going into all the chronological details here (I get more specific in my larger book, *End Time Delusions*), the prophecy starts with a direct *"commandment to restore and to build Jerusalem"* after the Babylonian captivity and reaches down to the first coming of Jesus Christ. After 69 weeks (after 483 years), *"shall Messiah be cut off."* All Christian scholars apply this to the crucifixion of Jesus Christ. After our Lord's agonizing death, "the people of the prince that shall come shall destroy the city and the sanctuary." While there are differences of opinion as to who "the people of the prince" refers to, the majority of scholars nevertheless apply the destruction of "the city and the sanctuary" to the second destruction of Jerusalem and its rebuilt sanctuary by Roman armies under Prince Titus in A.D. 70.

So far, we have seen 69 weeks fulfilled. That leaves "one week" left, otherwise known as the famous "70th week of Daniel." Again, that highly controversial text literally says:

And he shall confirm the covenant with many for one week: and in the midst of the week he shall cause the sacrifice and the oblation to cease... (Daniel 9:27 KJV).

Their idea is that while the first 69 weeks (or 483 years) did reach to the first coming of Jesus Christ, the prophetic clock has stopped because the Jewish people largely rejected Him.

Based on the day-year principle (which is valid), the "one week" remaining in this prophecy must refer to *a period of seven years*. Pro-rapture promoters claim this is the seven-year period of tribulation. Their idea is that while the first 69 weeks (or 483 years) did reach to the first coming of Jesus Christ, the prophetic clock has stopped because the Jewish people largely rejected Him. Then they slide the 70th week (the last seven years) all the way down to the end times, call it the tribulation, and say it applies to the Jewish people after we're gone.

Rapture teachers interpret Daniel 9:27 as follows:

1. "He shall confirm the covenant with many for one week." "He" is the antichrist who will make a covenant (or peace treaty) with the Jews during the seven years of tribulation.

2. "In the midst of the week he shall cause the sacrifice and the oblation to cease…" In the middle of the seven-year tribulation, the antichrist will break his covenant, turn against Israel, and stop their animal sacrifices.

3. The phrase, "he shall cause the sacrifice…to cease" is viewed as irrefutable proof that a Jewish temple (which includes sacrifices) *must* be rebuilt on the Temple Mount inside Jerusalem.

Bestselling author Hal Lindsey in his blockbuster *The Late Great Planet Earth* reflects this current view when he writes about "God's last seven years of dealing with the Jewish people before the long-awaited setting up of the kingdom of

God (see Daniel 9:27)."[1] According to Mr. Lindsey, during those seven years:

> "The Antichrist," breaks his covenant with the Jewish people and causes the Jewish temple worship, according to the Law of Moses, to cease (see Daniel 9:27)… We must conclude that a third Temple will be rebuilt upon its ancient site in old Jerusalem.[2]

…Daniel 9:27 says absolutely nothing about any seven-year tribulation, antichrist, or rebuilt Jewish temple!

In the same way, countless modern interpreters apply Daniel 9:27 to a future antichrist, a future peace treaty made with Israel, a future seven-year tribulation, and a future rebuilt Jewish temple inside Jerusalem. And all of this will supposedly start with the rapture. Honestly, that's a lot to interpret from that single verse, *especially when Daniel 9:27 says absolutely nothing about any seven-year tribulation, antichrist, or rebuilt Jewish temple!*

Could there be something wrong with this picture?

You'll find out in the next chapter.

Endnotes

1. Hal Lindsey, *The Late Great Planet Earth* (Grand Rapids, MI: Zondervan, 1977), 45-46.

2. Ibid., 46.

chapter 5

The 70th Week
of Daniel Delusion

*Truth is not determined
by majority vote.*
—Doug Gwyn

Prophecy-minded Christians all over planet Earth often engage in a fierce debate about whether Jesus Christ will return for His Church before the seven years of tribulation (the "pretrib" view), in the middle of the seven years (the "midtrib" view), or at the end of the seven years (the "post-trib" view). Yet by far the most explosive question too few seem to be asking is: "Is an end-time 'seven-year period of tribulation' really the correct interpretation of Daniel 9:27 in the first place?"

In 1945, after months of agonizing deliberation, U.S. President Harry Truman finally issued orders to drop two atomic bombs on Japan in an attempt to end World War II. On August 6, the "Little Boy" fell on Hiroshima. Three days later, the "Fat Man" was released over Nagasaki. Approximately 130,000 people were instantly vaporized. Many heated discussions have occurred as to whether it was the right thing to drop those bombs. One thing's for sure—in the minds of those who made that fearful decision, they believed it was for the ultimate good of America.

Dear friend, it is for the benefit of Christians everywhere that God's bomb of truth should now be released over what I have come to call "The 70th week of Daniel Delusion."

As we have already seen, Daniel 9:27 literally says:

He shall confirm the covenant with many for one week: and in the midst of the week he shall cause the sacrifice and the oblation to cease... (Daniel 9:27 KJV).

This may shock you, but historically, the vast majority of well-respected Bible scholars have not applied Daniel 9:27 to a seven-year period of tribulation at all. Neither have they interpreted the "he" as referring to a future Mr. Deadly. Instead, *they applied it to Jesus Christ.*

…historically, the vast majority of well-respected Bible scholars have not applied Daniel 9:27 to a seven-year period of tribulation at all.

Notice what the world-famous Bible commentary written by Matthew Henry says about Daniel 9:27: "By offering himself a sacrifice once and for all he [Jesus] shall put an end to all the Levitical sacrifices."[1] Thus Matthew Henry applied Daniel 9:27 to *Christ*, not the antichrist. Another famous commentary written by British Methodist Adam Clarke says that during Daniel 9:27's "term of seven years," Jesus Himself would "confirm or ratify the new covenant with mankind."[2] Another dusty Bible commentary reveals: "He shall confirm the covenant—Christ. The confirmation of the covenant is assigned to Him."[3]

Here's one more statement from a book called, *Christ and Antichrist*, published in 1846 by the Presbyterian Board of Publication in Philadelphia. On page two, under Recommendations, are endorsements from many Presbyterian, Methodist, and Baptist ministers, including an official representative of the Southern Baptist Convention.[4] Commenting on the final week of Daniel 9:27, that ancient volume states:

> ...sometime during the remaining seven, he [the Messiah] was to die as a sacrifice for sin, and thus bring in "everlasting righteousness." Here are allusions to events so palpable, that one would think, the people among whom they occurred, could not possibly have misapplied the prophecy.[5]

Okay, here we go. The following 10 points provide logical and convincing evidence that Daniel's famous 70th week has no application to any future seven-year tribulation at all. Rather, this great prophetic period was definitely fulfilled nearly 2,000 years ago.

1. The entire prophecy of Daniel 9:24-27 covers a period of "seventy weeks." Logic requires that "seventy weeks" refers to one consecutive block of time, in other words, to 70 *straight sequential weeks*. The truth is: there is no example in Scripture (or anywhere else!) of a stated time period starting, stopping, and then starting again. *All* biblical references to time are consecutive: 40

days and 40 nights, 400 years in Egypt, 70 years of captivity, and so on (see Gen. 7:4; 15:13; Dan. 9:2). In Daniel's prophecy, the "seventy weeks" were to begin during the reign of Persia and continue to the time of the Messiah.

…there is no example in Scripture (or anywhere else!) of a stated time period starting, stopping, and then starting again.

2. Logic also requires that the 70th week follow immediately after

the 69th week. If it doesn't, then it cannot properly be called the 70th week!

3. It is illogical to insert a 2,000-year gap between the 69th and 70th week. No hint of a gap is found in the prophecy itself. There is no gap between the first seven weeks and the following sixty-two weeks, so why insert one between the 69th and 70th week? (Note: If you told your child to be in bed in 70 minutes, you obviously would mean 70 *consecutive* minutes. What if five hours later your fully awake son said, "But Dad, I know 69 minutes have passed, but the 70th minute hasn't started yet"? After

receiving an appropriate punish-
ment, he would be swiftly sent to
bed.)

4. Daniel 9:27 says nothing about a
    seven-year period of "tribulation,"
    a "rebuilt" Jewish temple, or any
    "antichrist."

> **The stated focus of this
> prophecy is the Messiah,
> not the antichrist.**

5. The stated focus of this prophecy
    is the Messiah, not the antichrist.
    After the Messiah is "cut off"
    (referring to Christ's death), the

text says, "And the people of the prince who is to come shall destroy the city and the sanctuary." In the past, this has been consistently applied to the destruction of Jerusalem and the second temple by Roman armies led by Prince Titus in A.D. 70.[6]

The word *covenant* is Messianic, and *always* applies to the Messiah, not the antichrist.

6. *"He shall confirm the covenant."* Paul said, *"the covenant"* was *"confirmed before by God in Christ"* (Gal. 3:17). Jesus Christ came *"to*

confirm *the promises made to the fathers"* (Rom. 15:8). In the King James Version, Daniel 9:27 doesn't say "*a* covenant" or peace treaty, but "*the* covenant," which applies to the New Covenant. Nowhere in the Bible does the antichrist make, confirm, or break a covenant with anyone. The word *covenant* is Messianic, and *always* applies to the Messiah, not the antichrist.

7. "He shall confirm the *covenant* with *many*." Jesus Christ said, *"This is My blood of the new covenant, which is shed for **many…**"* (Matt. 26:28). Behold a perfect fit! Jesus was quoting Daniel 9:27 specifically.

8. "In the midst of the week he shall cause the sacrifice and the oblation to cease." After exactly three and a half years of holy ministry, Jesus Christ died on the Cross, "in the midst of the week [in the middle of the seven years]." At the exact moment of His death, *"the veil of the temple was torn in two from top to bottom..."* (Matt. 27:51). This act of God signified that all animal sacrifices at that moment ceased to be of value. Why? Because the Perfect Sacrifice had been offered!

9. *"For the overspreading of abominations he shall make it desolate."*

"The abomination of desolation" is not a simple subject (see Matt. 24:15). However, we know that Jesus clearly applied this event to the time when His followers were to flee from Jerusalem before the destruction of the second Temple in A.D. 70. In a parallel text to Matthew 24:15, Jesus told His disciples, *"When you see Jerusalem surrounded by armies* [Roman armies led by Prince Titus], *then know that its desolation is near"* (Luke 21:20). The disciples did "see" those very events. Because of the "abominations" of the Pharisees, Jesus told them,

"See! Your house is left to you desolate" (Matt. 23:38). Thus, Gabriel's statement in Daniel 9:27 about Jerusalem becoming "desolate" was perfectly fulfilled in A.D. 70.

Thus, approximately 3½ years after the crucifixion and at the end of the 70-week prophecy given for the Jewish people, the Gospel shifted to the Gentiles *exactly as predicted in Bible prophecy.*

10. Gabriel said that the 70-week prophecy specifically applied to the Jewish people (see Dan. 9:24). During the period of Christ's public ministry of 3½ years, the Master's focus was largely on *"the lost sheep of the house of Israel"* (Matt. 10:6). After His resurrection and then for another 3½ years, His disciples preached mostly to Jews (see Acts 1-6). After that second 3½-year period, in A.D. 34, the bold Stephen was stoned by the Jewish Sanhedrin (see Acts 7). This infamous deed marked the then-ruling Jewish leaders' final, official rejection of the Gospel of

our Savior. *Then* the Gospel went to the Gentiles. In Acts 9, Saul became Paul, the *"apostle to the Gentiles"* (Rom. 11:13). In Acts 10, God gave Peter a vision revealing it was *now time* to preach to the Gentiles (see Acts 10:1-28). Read also Acts 13:46. Thus, approximately 3½ years after the crucifixion and at the end of the 70-week prophecy given for the Jewish people, the Gospel shifted to the Gentiles *exactly as predicted in Bible prophecy.*

The explosive evidence is overwhelming. Point by point, the events of Daniel's 70th week have been fulfilled in the past. These eight words found in Daniel 9:27—"confirm, covenant, many, midst, sacrifice, cease, abominations, desolate"—all find perfect fulfillment in Jesus Christ and early Christian history.

In the words of that 1846 Presbyterian publication:

> "The *seventy weeks* of Daniel therefore, have certainly *ended* many centuries ago. We are not to look to the *future* for the fulfillment of these predictions. We must look to *the past*. And if to the past; where is there one who can have any adequate claims to being the subject of these prophecies, but *Jesus?* He, and he *only* can claim them; and

to him they most certainly refer."[7]

"...one would think, the people [the Jews] among whom [these events] occurred, could not possibly have misapplied the prophecy."[8]

Amazingly, the exact same thing is happening today. Sincere Christian scholars are now misapplying the very same prophecy.

But they did. In fact, one major reason why the Jewish nation as a whole failed to receive its Messiah was because its scholars misinterpreted Daniel 9:27. They failed to see Jesus Christ as the predicted One who would die in the midst of the 70th week! Amazingly, the exact same thing is happening today. Sincere Christian scholars are now mis-applying the very same prophecy.

The entire "seven-year period of tribulation" theory is a *rapture delusion*, a massive mega-myth. It may even go down in history as the "greatest evangelical misinterpretation of all time."[9] The whole concept is like a gigantic bubble. Once Daniel 9:27 is correctly understood and the sharply pointed pin of truth is inserted, "Pop goes the seven years!" It's a fact. There is no text in the Bible that teaches a "seven-year tribulation." If you hunt for it, you'll end up like Ponce de Leon searching for the mystical Fountain of Youth but never finding it.

Instead of basing our end-time convictions on what *isn't there,* I urge you to accept one of the most basic of all New Testament teachings that *is there*—the truth of the second coming of Jesus Christ.

The Master Himself predicted, *"For as the lightning comes from the east and flashes to the west, so also will the coming of the Son of Man be"* (Matt. 24:27).

On that Glorious Day, those who belong to King Jesus will receive new bodies, and become young forever (see 1 Cor. 15:52-55).

So don't be fooled about the future.

The consequences of believing lies can be quite debilitating.

Endnotes

1. Matthew Henry, *Commentary on the Whole Bible*, vol. IV (New York: Fleming H. Revell Co., 1712), 1094-1095.

2. Adam Clarke, *The Holy Bible With a Commentary and Critical Notes*, vol. IV (New York: Abingdon-Cokesbury Press, 1825), 602.

3. Rev. Robert Jamieson, A.R. Fausset, and Rev. David Brown, *A Commentary Critical and Explanatory on the Whole Bible* (Hartford, CT: S.S. Scranton Co., 1871), 641.

4. Rev. Samuel J. Cassels, *Christ and Antichrist* (Philadelphia: Presbyterian Board of Publication, 1846), 2.

5. *Ibid.*, 47.

6. See notes on Daniel 9:26 in Henry, *Commentary,* 1095; Clarke, *The Holy Bible,* 603; and Jamieson, Fausset, and Brown, *A Commentary,* 641.

7. Cassels, *Christ and Antichrist*, 49.

8. Ibid., 47.

9. Steve Wohlberg, *End Time Delusions* (New York: Treasure House, 2005), 47.

chapter 6

Hidden History
Hits the Headlines

*In an age of universal deceit,
telling the truth is a
revolutionary act.*
—George Orwell (1902-1950)

I remember the event as if it happened yesterday. There it sat, inside an airport newsstand in Atlanta. I didn't have much time to catch my connection to Canada, but the magazine cover grabbed my attention immediately. *Time* magazine, July 1, 2002. Flames surrounded a large cross with these words emblazoned: "*The Bible and the Apocalypse:* Why more Americans are reading and talking about *the end of the world.*"

I paid the $3.95.

On the plane I read the cover story titled "Apocalypse Now," highlighting the surge of American interest in deciphering biblical prophecies after the September 11 terrorist attack on the World Trade Center in New York City. Raptureready.com was featured, an incredibly popular Website whose Webmaster has invented a "Rapture Index," calling it a "Dow Jones Industrial

Average of End Time activity."[1] On September 24, 2001, 13 days after 9-11, the site's "bandwidth nearly melted under the weight of 8 million visitors."

The article's center spread showed full-color pictures of the entire *Left Behind* series, with the words "Copies Sold" written under each book: "*Left Behind*—7,000,000; *Tribulation Force*—4,100,000; *Desecration*—3,100,000" and so on. Below was a box labeled "Glossary of Terms" defining apocalyptic phraseology for the average Joe. I was especially interested to see how "The Tribulation" was defined: "A period of seven years of disaster that will end with Christ's defeat of evil at Armageddon."[2]

"Meet the Prophet" was the title of another four-page story a few pages in. Dead center was a large photograph of Tim LaHaye preaching, with "Taking his message to the masses," as the subheading. The next page showed Jerry B. Jenkins standing next to a sidebar picturing "*Left Behind* Wares" including comic books, a kids series, and a Monopoly-style *Left Behind* board game. All of these *Time* articles described a heightened interest in prophecy—especially among evangelical Christians—and spelled out the popular views being critiqued in this book: rapture first, seven-year tribulation next, during which Mr. Wicked appears and attacks the Jews.

Except for one article. Page 46. Its intriguing title was *The End: How It Got That Way* by journalist David Van Biema. My heart started pounding. *Could it be?* Below the headline was a little picture (maybe 1 by 1.5 inches, smaller than those of LaHaye, Jenkins, and each *Left Behind* book) of a curious-looking man by the name of John Nelson Darby, who lived in England during the 1800s. An obvious student of history, Van Biema referred to Mr. Darby as "the man with the plan" to introduce into nineteenth-century British and American Christianity "a radical new eschatology," which included believing in "a seven-year, hell-like Tribulation."

I could scarce believe my eyes. *Has some of the hidden history behind the historical development of the rapture doctrine actually surfaced in the mainstream press?* I wondered.

Amazingly, indeed it had.

Darby's contribution to the development of evangelical theology has been so great that he is even universally credited as being "The Father of Modern Dispensationalism."

Before quoting one key paragraph from Van Biema's insightful pen, I should clarify that John Nelson Darby (1800-1882) is no small fry in church history. Pastor, evangelist, lawyer, theologian, and the leader of group called The Plymouth Brethren, Darby wrote at least 53 books on Bible subjects. His ideas were so influential that in the early 1900s they were injected by Cyrus Scofield into his legendary Scofield Reference Bible, which brought them into mainstream American Protestant Bible schools and beyond. Darby's contribution to the development of evangelical theology has been so great that he is even universally credited as being "The Father of Modern Dispensationalism."

With these facts in mind, notice carefully these shocking sentences from reporter Van Biema in that July 1, 2002 issue of *Time* magazine:

> His [J.N. Darby's] most striking innovation was the timing of a concept called the Rapture, drawn from the Apostle Paul's prediction that believers would fly up to meet Christ in Heaven. Most theologians understood it as part of the Resurrection at time's very end, Darby repositioned it at the Apocalypse's very beginning, a small shift with large implications. It spared true believers the Tribulation, leaving the horror to nonbelievers and the doctrinally misled...Darby's scheme became a pillar of the new Fundamentalism.[3]

...the Rapture doctrine
was really only John
Nelson Darby's "most
striking innovation."

There it is! I thought to myself. *Even though* Time *magazine is a liberal publication, the truth has finally been told.* Van Biema is absolutely correct. Based on solid historical research, he accurately reported to millions of *Time* readers that the Rapture doctrine was really only John Nelson Darby's "most striking innovation." As Van Biema stated, Darby took Paul's "caught up" phrase in First Thessalonians 4:17 and then creatively "repositioned it at the Apocalypse's very beginning, a small shift with large implications." Significantly, Van Biema also noted that in the early 1800s, "most theologians" didn't see it that way, which is 100 percent correct. In fact, they had never heard of it. Yet as the decades wore on—like a theological terrorist destined to hijack popular Christian ideas about the end times—"Darby's scheme became a pillar of the new Fundamentalism."

No matter what pro-Rapture teachers adamantly claim, the biggest problem is that "Darby's scheme" and "most striking innovation" isn't truly biblical. After reading this book, hopefully, you can discern this.

Now you know a bit of the history behind the origin of the Rapture doctrine and who helped make it popular. For more information, I recommend my larger book, *End Time Delusions,* and also Dave MacPherson's controversial *The Rapture Plot* and *The Incredible Cover-Up: Exposing the Origins of Rapture Theories.*

As we near the end of *The Rapture Delusion,* the bottom line is that God's Word doesn't really teach "rapture-tribulation-end" at all. Daniel's 70th week is history and true believers will be "caught up" at the loud, visible second coming of Jesus Christ, rather than seven years before it.

The most important question of all is—will you be ready? I hope so. I long to be ready, too.

The most important question of all is—will you be ready?

Dear reader, it's obvious that biblical prophecies are being fulfilled all around us, including Paul's prediction that many, even within the Church, would *"turn their ears away from the truth, and be turned aside to fables"* (2 Tim. 4:4). In the midst of global religious confusion and increasing economic woes, the One who died on a cruel Cross to pay the price for our waywardness now beckons earnestly, *"Follow Me and My Book!"* *"And you shall know the truth,"* He promises, *"and the truth shall make you free"* (John 8:32).

Yes, Jesus Christ is coming soon, and when He appears, there will be nothing silent or secret about that earth-shaking event. Instead of millions of head-scratching secularists wondering where all the Christians went, it will be the Big Day, and everyone will know it.

Now is the time to prepare our hearts and our families for the loud, cataclysmic, visible return of our Lord and Savior Jesus Christ, who passionately loves us and who longs to live with us forever—even forever and ever.

Now is the time to prepare our hearts and our families for the loud, cataclysmic, visible return of our Lord and Savior Jesus Christ,...

The hour is late.

This is no time to be "caught up" in innovations, novels, and movies like *Left Behind.*

Endnotes

1. Nancy Gibbs, "Apocalypse Now," Time, July 1, 2002, 43.

2. Ibid., 45.

3. Ibid., 46.

ADDITIONAL RESOURCES
WITH STEVE WOHLBERG

End Time Delusions
(hardcover, paperback, and DVD)

The Ultimate Passover **(DVD)**

Islam Revisited **(DVD)**

Demons in Disguise: The Dangers of Talking to the Dead **(paperback)**

The Trouble With Twilight: Why Today's Vampire Craze Is Hazardous to Your Health **(paperback)**

To order, contact
White Horse Media
P.O. Box 1139
Newport, WA 99156
1 (800) 782-4253
Visa/MasterCard Accepted

Steve Wohlberg's solid Bible teaching is influencing people around the world. To learn more about his television and radio ministry, visit www.whitehorsemedia.com.

Additional copies of this book and other
book titles from DESTINY IMAGE are
available at your local bookstore.

Call toll-free: 1-800-722-6774.

Send a request for a catalog to:

Destiny Image® Publishers, Inc.

P.O. Box 310
Shippensburg, PA 17257-0310

*"Speaking to the Purposes of God for This
Generation and for the Generations to Come."*

**For a complete list of our titles,
visit us at www.destinyimage.com.**